GENERAL INSTRUCTION

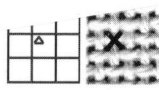
This design is worked on **evenweave** fabric, using cross stitch, back stitch and long straight stitches.

THE THREAD

Each length of thread consists of six strands. You will stitch with two strands or one strand for this design. For some of the work you will need to put together one strand of one colour and one strand of another colour to obtain the required effect.

Fasten on and off by passing the thread under stitches on the back of your work. Do not use knots and do not make large jumps on the back of your work.

THE STITCHES

Cross Stitch

Your chart is made up of squares containing a symbol or symbols. Each symbol represents a colour which is described on the colour key. Each square on the chart represents the space required to work a whole cross, i.e. two threads of the fabric. If there is only one symbol in the square a cross will be worked like this:

Work crosses in a line where possible. Make sure that all the top diagonal stitches lie in the same direction or the crosses will look higgledy piggledy and will spoil your picture.

Sometimes symbols straddle the lines of the graph. The stitch is worked just the same as usual, but one thread of the fabric out of line with the normal stitches in the design.

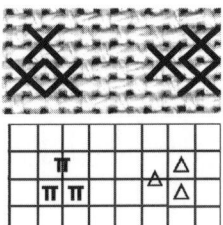

Half stitches

Remember that each square on the chart takes up the same amount of room, so if there are two symbols together in a square the stitches made will take up the same amount of room as a whole cross.

Horizontal half stitches   Vertical half stitches

These diagrams illustrate how half stitches are shown and worked.

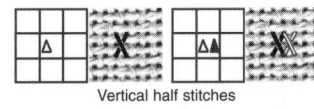

Diagonal half stitches

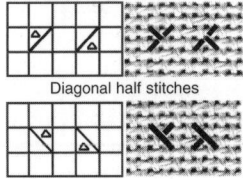

Where two diagonal half stitches are together in one square work both fully, making the two long diagonal stitches lie side by side.

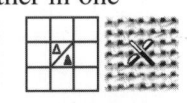

Quarter stitches

A quarter stitch takes u... the whole cross, and it... square.

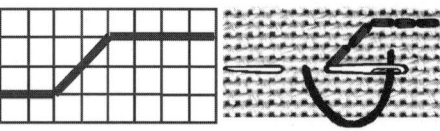

Outlining stitches

Outlining is worked in back stitch and long stitches as indicated in the colour key. They are worked like this:

Back stitch

Long stitch

Sometimes you will need to work through the middle of a cross and you may find this easier to do if you use a needle with a sharp point.

BEFORE YOU START

To prevent your fabric from fraying, edge with a whipping stitch, a zig zag stitch on a sewing machine or protect with masking tape. You may wish to use a hoop. If you do, bind it first to prevent it from marking the fabric.

THE RIVER THAMES CHARTS

This design has been split up into six separate charts, each with an overlap with the next. A diagram showing the layout of these charts is on page 2. Each chart shows the cross stitch and main outlining required. The outlining for each building is shown separately, together with information about the building.

You may wish to add extra features to your map. Page 13 includes ideas for these and ways in which you might like to adapt parts of the map for other purposes. Finishing and framing instructions are also included on page 13.

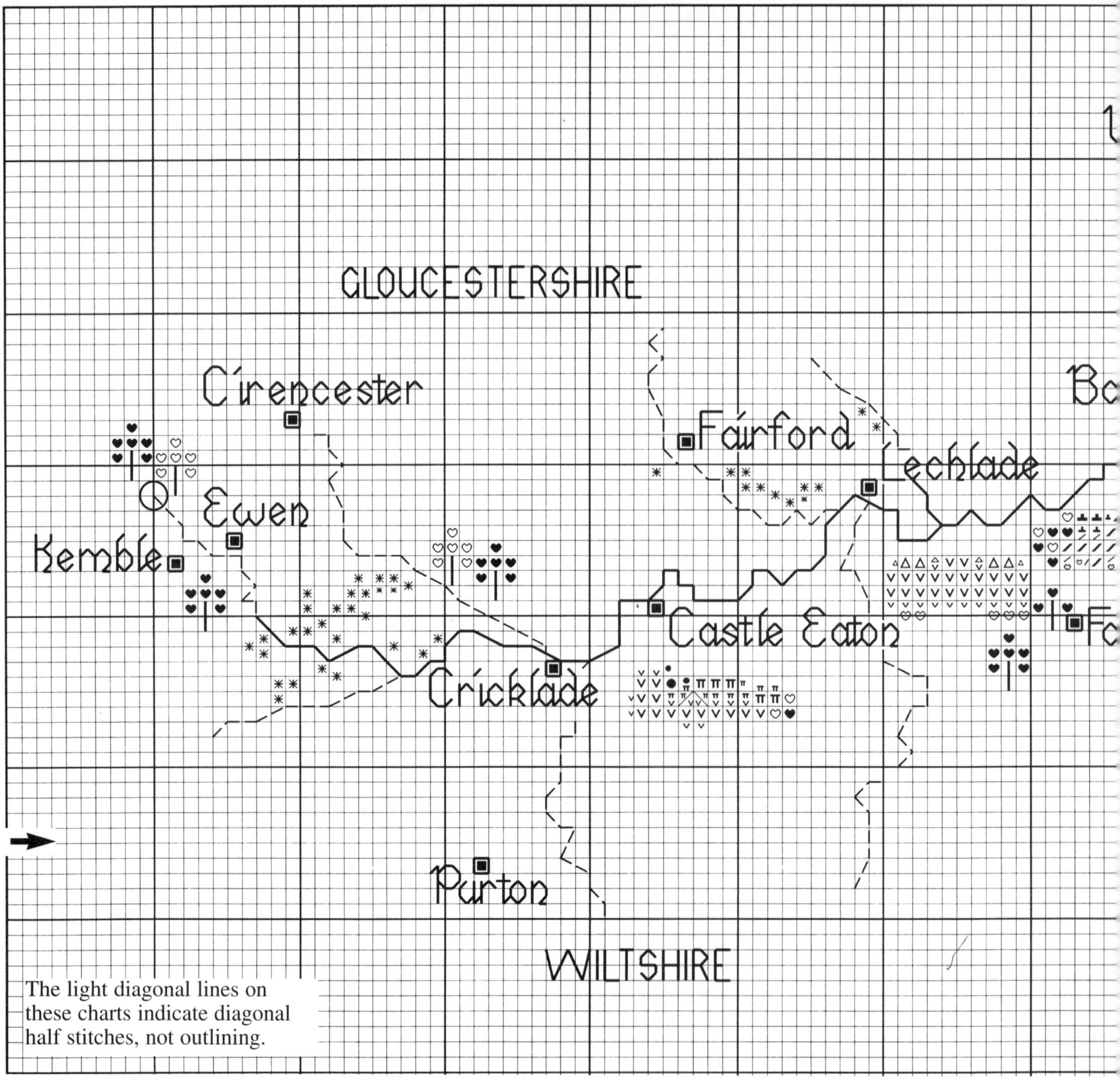

The chart shows a cross-stitch map with the following place names:

GLOUCESTERSHIRE

Cirencester

Fairford

Lechlade

Bo

Ewen

Kemble

Castle Eaton

Fo

Cricklade

Purton

WILTSHIRE

The light diagonal lines on these charts indicate diagonal half stitches, not outlining.

The charts for this design are laid out as follows:

The River Thames

Page 8   Page 10   Page 11

Page 2   Page 4   Page 6   Page 12

Materials required for this map of the River Thames

Fabric

27 or 28 count evenweave fabric size 41" x 15" (104 cms. x 38 cms.)
We have used Zweigart 27 count 'linda' in ivory on which the design size of the picture is 33" x 8½" (83 cms. x 21.5 cms.)

Needle - Tapestry size 24 or 26

Stranded Cottons

DMC stranded cottons have been used for this design and all the references on the charts are for these. They are listed on page 3 together with suggested alternative Anchor and Madeira colours - however, these may not be perfect matches.

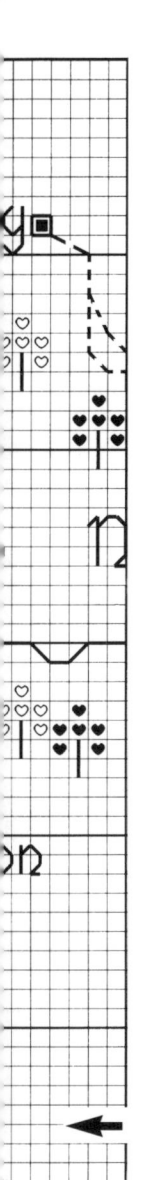

DMC-Anchor-Madeira			DMC-Anchor- Madeira		
301	-349 -	2305 (2)	793	-176 -	0906 (4)
310	-403 -	2400 (12)	794	-175 -	0907 (2)
402	-1047-	2307 (1)	839	-359 -	1914 (2)
415	-398 -	1802 (2)	841	-378 -	1911 (2)
453	-231 -	1806 (2)	842	-376 -	1910 (1)
543	-933 -	1909 (1)	844	-273 -	1810 (6)
✓640	-393 -	1905 (1)	935	-269 -	1507 (1)
✓642	-392 -	1903 (2)	3021	-905 -	1904 (4)
✓644	-391 -	1902 (2)	3033	-390 -	1907 (3)
646	-235 -	1811 (2)	3064	-883 -	2312 (2)
647	-399 -	1812 (1)	3072	-274 -	1805 (1)
648	-234 -	1813 (1)	✓3347	-266 -	1408 (5)
738	-361 -	2013 (2)	3348	-264 -	1409 (5)
739	-276 -	2014 (2)	✓white-2	-	2401 (2)
792	-177 -	0913 (12)			

The numbers in brackets refer to the number of 2 foot (60 cm.) six strand lengths required.

Preparation

1. Tack a line of stitches along the centre of the fabric to mark the HORIZONTAL middle line. Use a light colour to make this line - a darker colour may leave a mark on your fabric. This line will correspond to that marked by arrows on the charts and will help you to check that your stitches are in the correct position as you work.

2. You are going to start stitching at the source of the River Thames. Thread your needle with one strand of 792 (dark blue) cotton. From the left hand side of your fabric measure 4½" (11 cms.) along your line of tacking stitches and count up 46 threads of the material (23 squares on the chart). This is the position marked with a circle on the chart, the start of the hyphenated line representing the start of the river. Check this position again to make sure that you are in the right place, and you can begin stitching your map.

The River Thames from Kemble to Brampton

The official source of the Thames is at Thameshead in Trewsbury Mead, about three miles west of Cirencester, Gloucestershire. The spring is visible only in winter.

Castle Eaton was once a fortification guarding a crossing of the river. Its church is pictured on the map.

Buscot Park is two miles south-east of Lechlade. The house was originally built in the 1780s, but greatly altered in Victorian times. It was restored by the second Lord Faringdon in the 1930s, and with nearly 4,000 acres is owned by the National Trust.

At Lechlade the River Leach joins the Thames. At St. John's lock near here is the first lock on the river - the Thames is officially navigable.

Kelmscott Manor is some two miles below Buscot. William Morris made his home there from 1871 until his death in 1896. He called the manor 'a heaven on earth'.

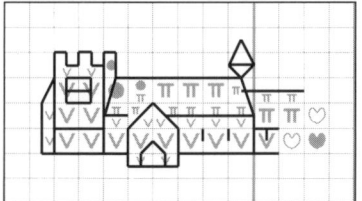

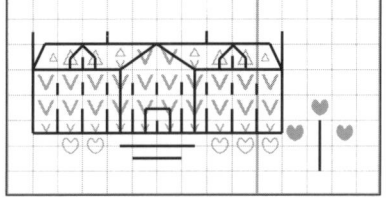

Cross stitch using two strands of cotton
- ■ 310 (black)
- △ 415 (medium blue grey)
- ● 646 (dark grey)
- ╱ 739 (light gold)
- ♥ 3347 (medium green)
- ♡ 3348 (light green)

Using one strand of cotton
- ✱ 792 (dark blue)

Cross stitch using one strand of each of two colours
- π 646 (dk. grey) and 3033 (fawn)
- ⊥ 739 (lt. gold) and 3021 (brown)
- v 739 (lt. gold) and 3033 (fawn)

Place Markers
- ■ The cross is worked with two strands of black cotton and then outlined with one strand. To save re-threading your needle use one strand, going over each diagonal of the cross twice before outlining.

Outlining for lettering
One strand of 310 (black). Work in back stitch, frequently over one thread of the fabric.

Outlining for rivers
- - - - - -one strand of 792 (dk.blue)
- ————two strands of 792 (dk.blue)

Work in back stitch

Outlining for buildings
Outline buildings and features in back stitch using one strand of 844 (charcoal).

Outlining for tree trunks
Two strands of 3021 (brown) working in back stitch.

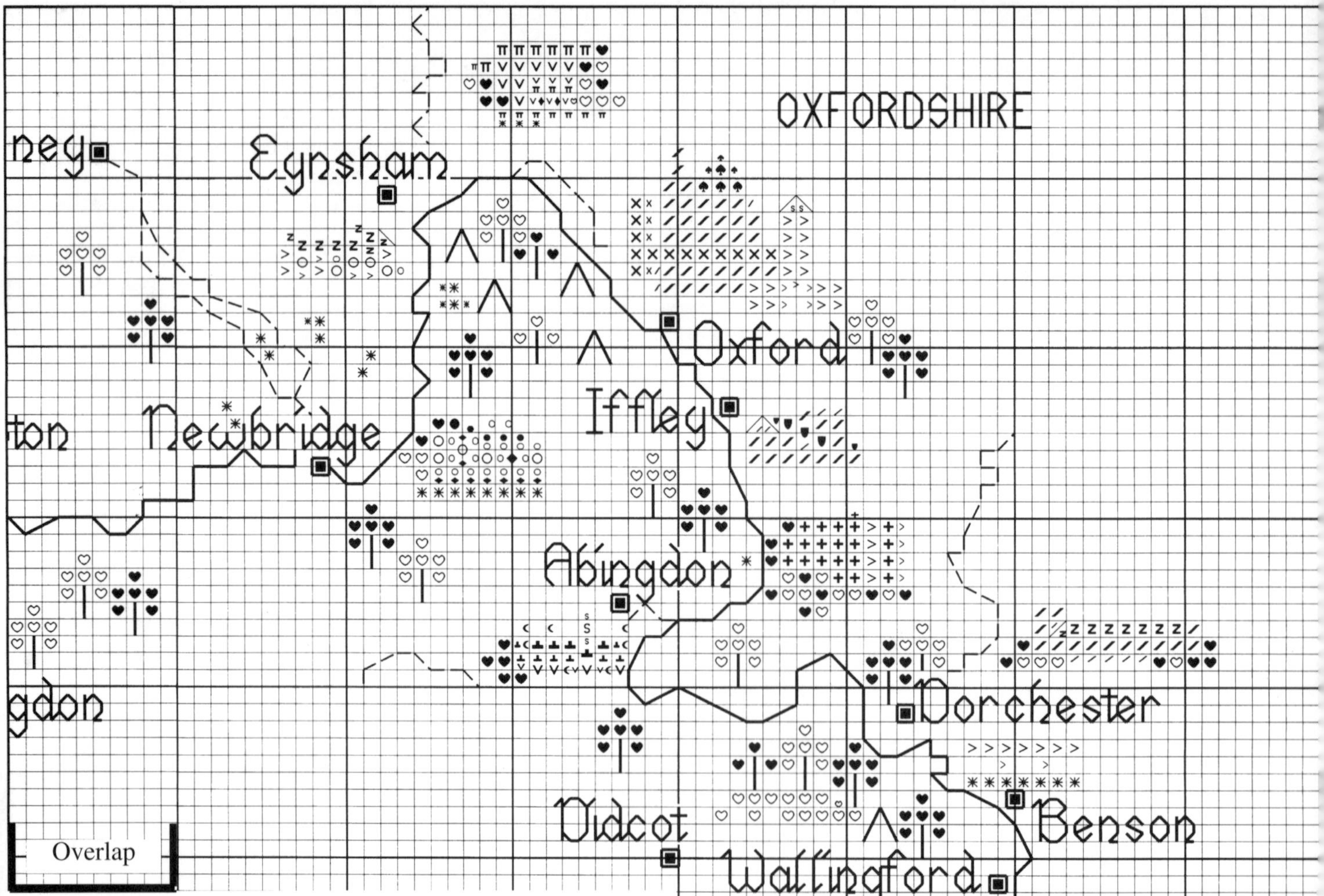

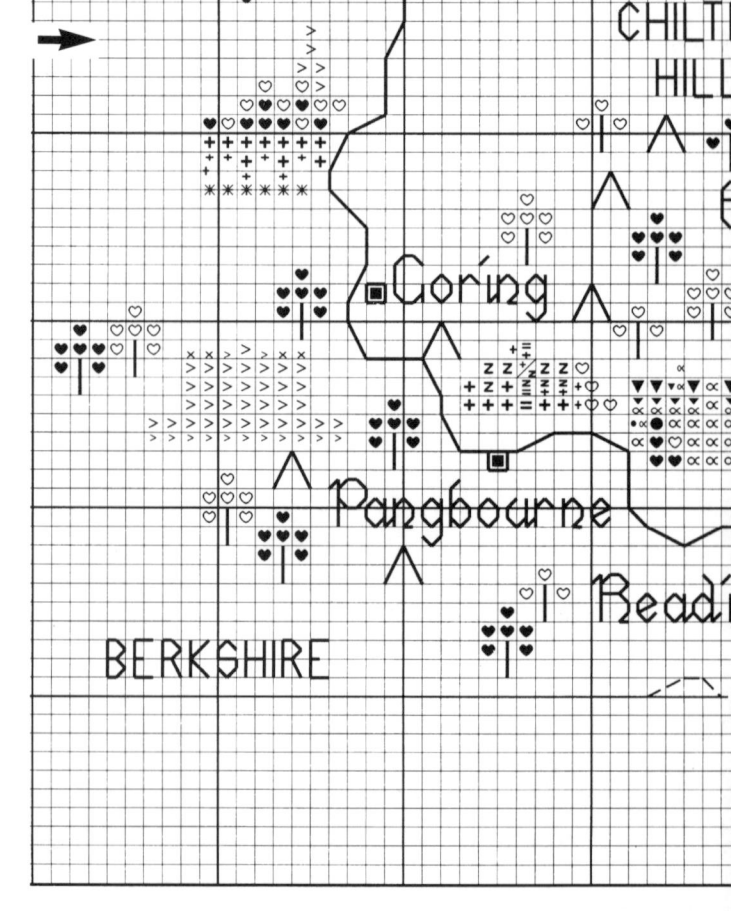

OXFORDSHIRE

ney■

Egynsham

ton Newbridge

gdon

Oxford

Iffley

Abingdon

Didcot

Wallingford

Dorchester

Benson

CHILTE
HILL

Goring

Pangbourne

Readi

BERKSHIRE

Cross stitch using two strands of cotton

- ■ 310 (black)
- = 402 (copper)
- × 453 (lt. red grey)
- ＋ 644 (lt. brown grey)
- ● 646 (dark grey)
- ♠ 648 (medium grey)
- ╱ 739 (lt. gold)
- ◆ 844 (charcoal)
- > 3033 (fawn)
- ᴄ 3064 (lt. red brown)
- s 3072 (lt. grey)
- ♥ 3347 (medium green)
- ♡ 3348 (lt. green)
- o White

Cross stitch using one strand of each of two colours

- ♥ 543 (lt. red grey) and 3021 (brown)
- z 640 (dk. brown grey) and 642 (brown grey)
- π 646 (dark grey) and 3033 (fawn)
- ∝ 738 (gold) and 842 (light pink brown)
- ▼ 738 (gold) and 3064 (lt. red brown)
- ⊥ 739 (lt. gold) and 3021 (brown)
- v 739 (lt. gold) and 3033 (fawn)

Cross stitch using one strand of cotton

- ✳ 792 (dark blue)

Outlining for lettering
One strand of 310 (black).

Outlining for rivers
- - - - - one strand of 792 (dark blue)
───── two strands of 792 (dark blue)

Outlining for buildings
One strand of 844 (charcoal)

Outlining for Tree trunks
Two strands of 3021 (brown)

Outlining for Hills
∧ Two strands of 301 (bronze), working in back stitch

The light diagonal lines on these charts indicate diagonal half stitches, not outlining.

Overlap

The River Thames from Newbridge to Pangbourne

A medieval bridge spans both the Thames and its tributary, the Windrush at Newbury.

Near Eynsham is Swinford toll bridge, one of the two bridges over the Thames where tolls are still charged. The other is at Whitchurch. The toll-house is pictured on the map.

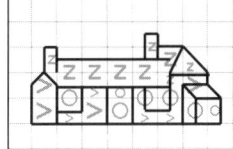

This is the Ferry Inn at Bablock Hythe. It was here that Matthew Arnold wrote of the Scholar Gypsy crossing the stripling Thames.

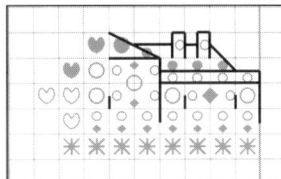

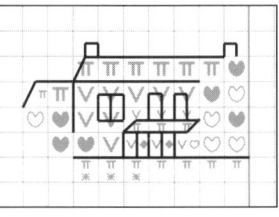

The Trout Inn is on the edge of Oxford.

An impressive group of buildings mark the university city of Oxford. Tom Tower is part of Christ Church College, founded by Wolsey in 1525. The Radcliffe Camera is the finest example of a circular library in England. Degrees were once conferred at the University Church of St. Mary the Virgin. Magdalen College was founded by the Bishop of Winchester in 1458.

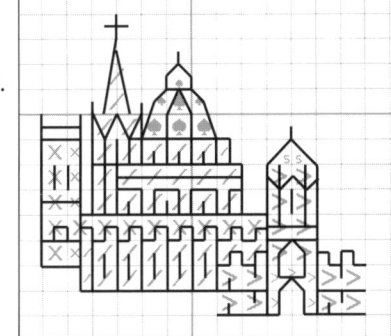

St. Mary's Church, Iffley is considered to be one of the best preserved 12th-century village churches in England.

Five miles below Iffley is Nuneham House, originally built by the first Lord Harcourt in 1756. Its park, now owned by the University of Oxford, is the work of Capability Brown and William Mason. The village of Nuneham Courtney is a notable example of an 18th-century model village.

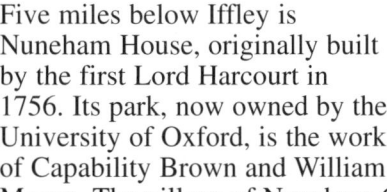

These almshouses are at Abingdon, a mainly 18th-century market town.

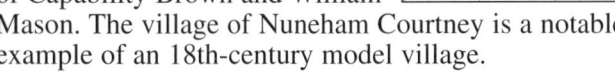
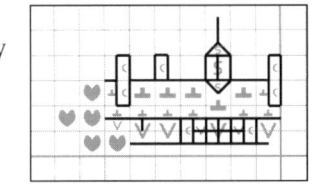

People have lived in Abingdon since the early Stone Age and among its other notable buildings are the Abbey dating from the 7th century, the 17th-century County Hall and the Old Gaol, which stands by the river.

At the Barley Mow Inn at Clifton Hampden, below Abingdon, Jerome K. Jerome wrote part of 'Three Men in a Boat'.

For centuries Dorchester was one of the most important towns in the whole of the Thames valley. It commands the junction of the Thame

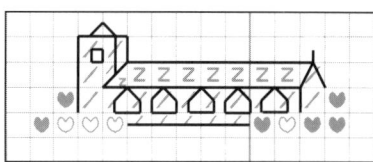

and the Thames. The Abbey Church of St. Peter and St. Paul is pictured on the map.

The group of trees on the map to the right of Didcot represents Wittenham Clumps. Here is an Iron Age hill-fort.

Shillingford Bridge was built in 1826 at the time when horse-drawn road transport, particularly coaching, was at its peak.

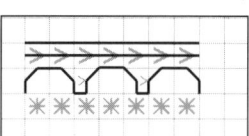

At Wallingford is a curious bridge with seventeen arches. It was originally medieval, but rebuilt in 1809. Wallingford grew to great importance because of its position on the Thames and because of its ford, being bigger than Cambridge in the time of Domesday. St. Peter's Church, pictured here with the bridge dates from 1777 and has an openwork spire.

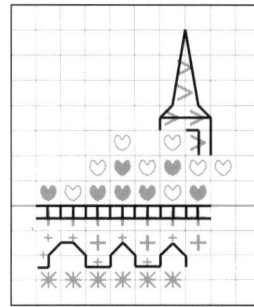

Above Goring, the Beetle and Wedge at Moulsford is said to be the model for the Potwell Inn in H.G. Wells's novel 'The History of Mr. Polly'.

The River Thames makes its way between the chalk hills of the Chilterns and the Berkshire Downs at Goring Gap. From Goring to Henley the Thames runs through the Chilterns Area of Outstanding Natural Beauty.

Basildon Park was built in 1776, and is rated as the most splendid Georgian mansion of Berkshire.

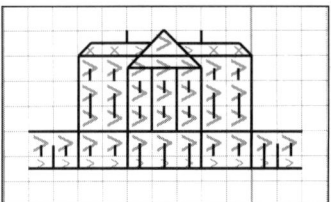

The mill at Mapledurham is one of the oldest surviving corn-mills on the Thames. It was this stretch of the river which became the setting for Kenneth Graham's 'Wind in the Willows'.

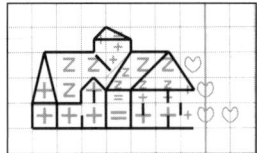

5

Cross stitch using two strands of cotton

- ■ 310 (black)
- △ 415 (med. blue grey)
- ⋏ 640 (dk. brown grey)
- ⧧ 642 (beige)
- ✛ 644 (lt. brown grey)
- ● 646 (dark grey)
- ♠ 648 (medium grey)
- ╱ 739 (lt. gold)
- ◆ 844 (charcoal)
- ＞ 3033 (fawn)
- ℂ 3064 (lt. red brown)
- ♥ 3347 (med. green)
- ♡ 3348 (lt. green)
- ○ White

Using one strand of cotton

- ✳ 792 (dark blue)

Using one strand of each of two colours

- ∟ 648 (med. grey) and white

- ▼ 738 (gold) and 3064 (red brown)
- π 646 (dark grey) and 3033 (fawn)
- ∼ 3072 (lt. grey) and white
- ∝ 738 (gold) and 842 (lt. brown)
- ⊥ 739 (lt. gold) and 3021 (brown)
- Ⅴ 647 (grey) and 3064 (red brown)
- z 640 (brown grey) and 642 (beige)

Outlining for lettering
One strand of 310

Outlining for rivers
- - - - - one strand of 792
_____ two strands of 792

Outlining for buildings
One strand of 844

Outlining for tree trunks
Two strands of 3021

Follow the chart at the bottom of page 8 to complete the title of this map

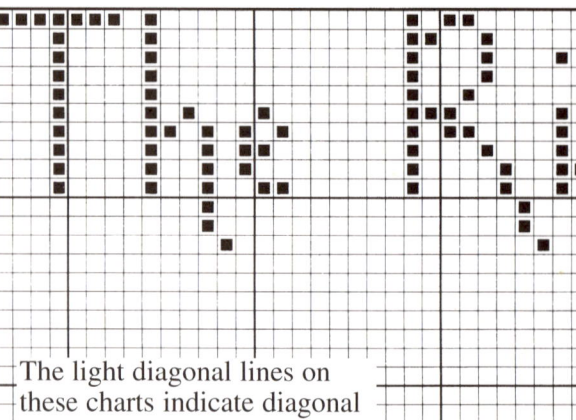

The light diagonal lines on these charts indicate diagonal half stitches, not outlining

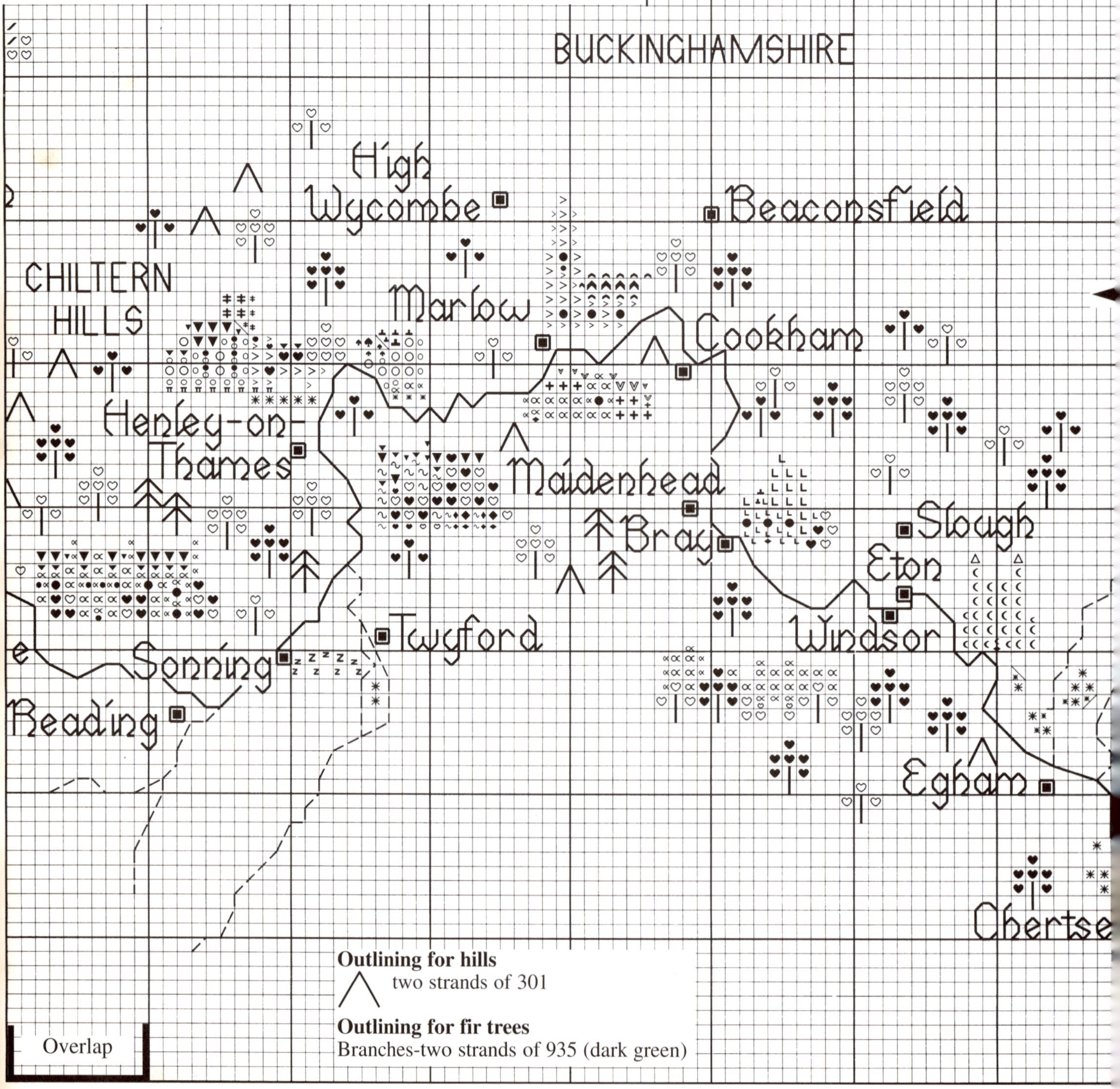

BUCKINGHAMSHIRE

High Wycombe · Beaconsfield

CHILTERN HILLS

Marlow · Cookham

Henley-on-Thames

Maidenhead

Bray · Slough

Eton

Twyford · Windsor

Sonning

Reading · Egham

Chertse

Outlining for hills
⋀ two strands of 301

Outlining for fir trees
Branches-two strands of 935 (dark green)

Overlap

The River Thames from Pangbourne to Egham

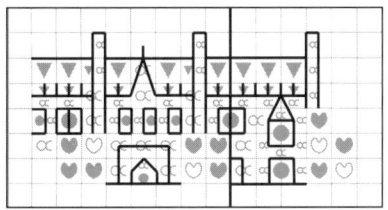

One of the most distinguished Elizabethan houses on the Thames is Mapledurham House. It dates from 1585, when it was built for Sir Richard Blount.

The university town of Reading is situated on the River Kennet near its confluence with the Thames. King Henry I was buried at Reading Abbey, of which very little remains.

Sonning has a picturesque bridge and many old houses. Sonning Lock is very attractive.

A well known Thames scene is the one of Henley-on-Thames which is pictured on the map. It features the Angel Inn, the 16th-century tower of St. Mary's Church and the bridge of 1786. Henley Royal Regatta, which dates from 1839, takes place at the beginning of July each year.

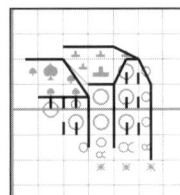

Hambleden Mill stands by Hambleden weir where canoeing is a favourite sport.

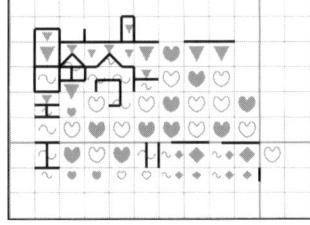

Medmenham Abbey dates from 1595. It was here that from about 1745 Sir Francis Dashwood ran the Hellfire Club.

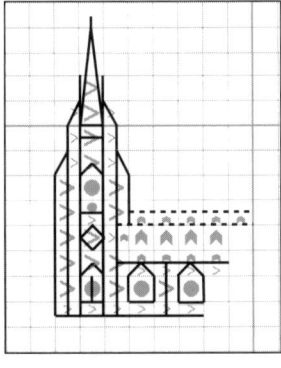

Marlow's 19th-century All Saints Church is pictured here. A suspension bridge crosses the Thames here. It is by William Tierney Clark and dates from 1831-6. Outline the roofs of the church (indicated by a dotted line) with one strand of 402 (bronze) using long stitches.

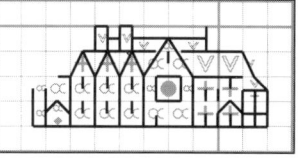

Bisham Abbey belonged in succession to the Templars, the Augustinians and the Benedictines before the Dissolution of the monasteries. In 1553 it became the property of Sir Philip Hoby. It is now a National Sports Centre where canoeing is among the many sports available. Bisham Abbey also incorporates the national training centre of the Lawn Tennis Association.

Boulter's Lock at Maidenhead is a boating rendezvous. Also at Maidenhead is Brunel's Great Western Railway bridge of 1837-8. Its semi-elliptical arch is 128 feet wide and claims to be the widest brick span in the world.

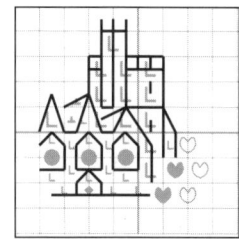

The 14th-century church of St. Michael at Bray is famous for its connection with the 18th-century song 'The Vicar of Bray' about the vicar who changed his religion depending on which king or queen was on the throne.

Every July the 'Swan-uppers' row from Sunbury to Pangbourne, counting and marking the season's cygnets. The beaks of Dyer's cygnets are marked with one nick, the Vintners' with two, and the Sovereign's are left unmarked.

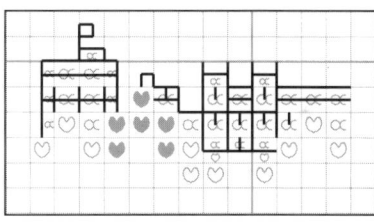

Windsor Castle has been a home of British monarchs for almost nine hundred years. It covers twelve acres and is the biggest castle in England and among the strongest. William the Conqueror began building it, and it has been enlarged by many sovereigns since. The Royal Windsor Horse Show is held in May on the meadows by the Thames below the Castle. Burford Lodge in St. Alban's Street was the home of Nell Gwynn.

Henry VI founded Eton College in 1440 under the title 'The King's College of Our Lady of Eton beside Windsor'. The brick gatehouse, pictured here, dates from about 1517.

Near Egham, between Windsor and Staines is Runnymede, a broad riverside meadow where the Magna Carta was sealed by King John in 1215.

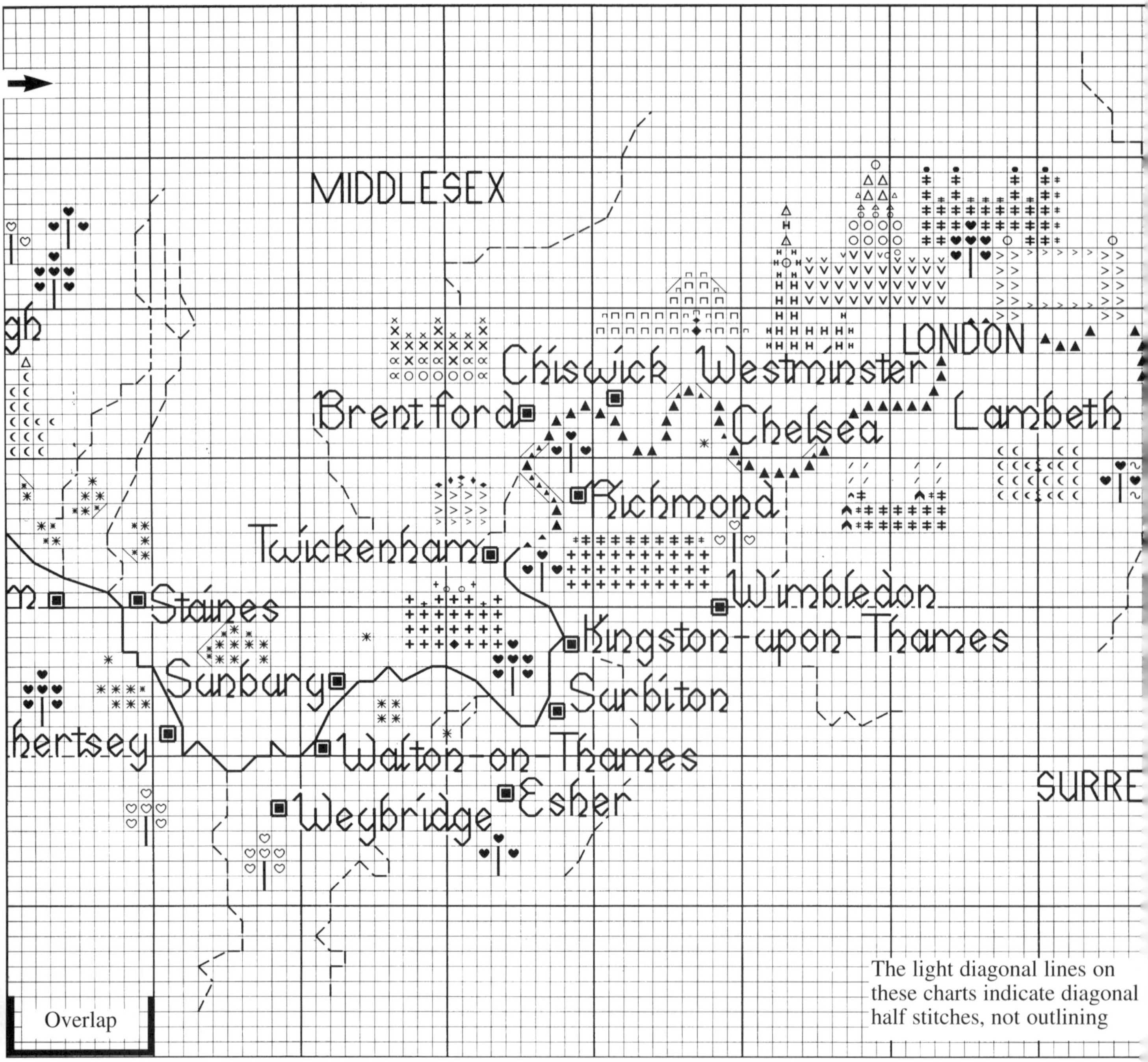

MIDDLESEX

LONDON

Chiswick Westminster

Brentford Chelsea Lambeth

Richmond

Twickenham

Staines Wimbledon

Kingston-upon-Thames

Sunbury Surbiton

hertsey Walton-on-Thames

SURRE

Weybridge Esher

The light diagonal lines on
these charts indicate diagonal
half stitches, not outlining

Overlap

**Cross stitch using two
strands of cotton**
- ■ 310 (black)
- △ 415 (blue grey)
- ✕ 453 (lt. red grey)
- ▲ 640 (dk. brown grey)
- ‡ 642 (beige)
- + 644 (lt. brown grey)
- ● 646 (dark grey)
- ╱ 739 (lt. gold)
- ▲ 792 (dark blue)
- H 842 (lt. pink brown)

- ◆ 844 (charcoal)
- > 3033 (fawn)
- ℂ 3064 (lt. red brown)
- ♥ 3347 (med. green)
- ♡ 3348 (lt. green)
- ○ White

Using one strand of cotton
- ✳ 792 (dark blue)

**Cross stitch using one strand
of each of two colours**
- ⊓ 415 (blue grey) and 3072
  (lt. grey)
- ∝ 738 (gold) and 842 (lt.
  pink brown)
- v 739 (lt. gold) and 3033
  (fawn)
- ~ 3072 (lt. grey) and white

Outlining for lettering
One strand of 310

Outlining for rivers
- - - - - - - one strand of 792
———— two strands of 792

Outlining for buildings
One strand of 844

Outlinig for tree trunks
Two strands of 3021

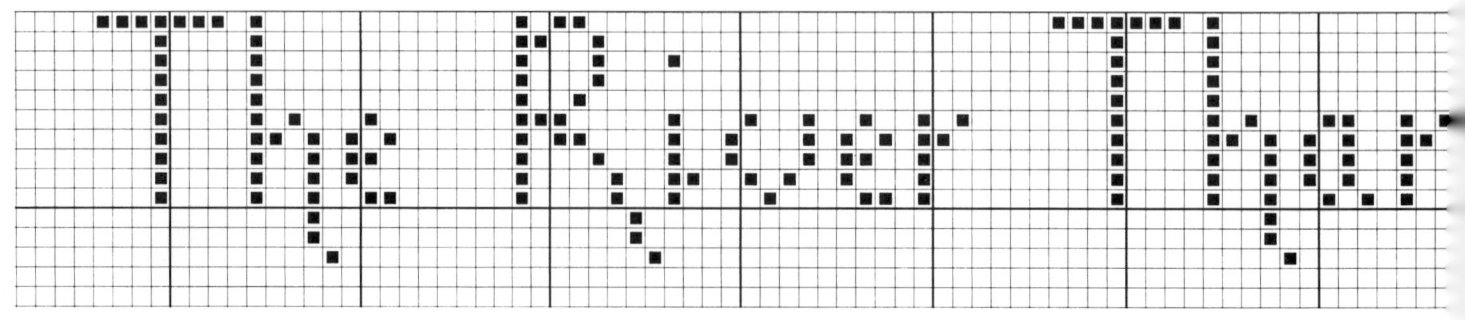

The River Thames from Egham to Greenwich

The area along the Thames near Staines is made up of water parks consisting of reservoirs and flooded gravel pits.

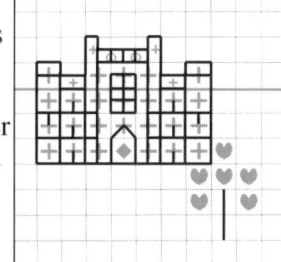

Hampton Court Palace was built by Cardinal Wolsey from 1515 but given to Henry VIII in 1525 in order to placate him. It became a favourite royal residence for the next two centuries.

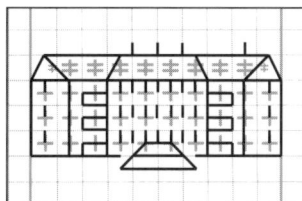

Ham House, now owned by the National Trust, was acquired by the Duke and Duchess of Lauderdale in the 17th century.

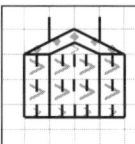

Marble Hill House was built by George II for his mistress, Henrietta Howard.

Richmond has many royal associations. Richmond Palace was built by Henry VII, and Henry VIII lived there with Katharine of Aragon. Elizabeth I, who was born at Greenwich Palace, died at Richmond Palace.

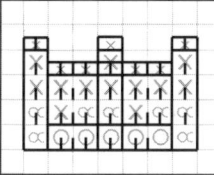

Syon House was given to the Earl of Northumberland by James I in the early 17th century and it has remained a home of the Percy family ever since.

The Great Palm House at the Royal Botanic Gardens, Kew was built from 1844-8. The Gardens, of great importance in the fields of education and research, were set up under Sir Joseph Hooker in 1840 and are a delight to their millions of yearly visitors.

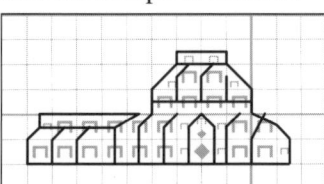

At Brentford the Grand Union Canal and the River Brent enter the Thames. It was at Brentford that Edmond Ironside successfully fought the Danes in 1016 and the Royalists defeated the Parliamentarians during the Civil War.

The Oxford and Cambridge Boat Race, first held at Henley in 1829, has since 1845 been rowed from Putney to Mortlake, a distance of $4^{1}/_{2}$ miles.

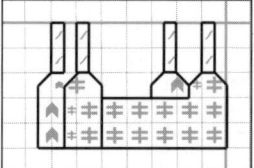

The striking landmark of Battersea Power Station was built by Gilbert Scott in 1932.

A group of famous buildings represents London. The Houses of Parliament, from where the nation is governed, was built after the old Palace of Westminster was destroyed by fire in 1834. Its clocktower houses Big Ben. Buckingham Palace was built in 1705 and bought by George III in 1761. In 1837 it was made the official London residence of the court by Queen Victoria, and it has remained as such to the present day. The dome of St. Paul's Cathedral is the third largest in the world. The Cathedral, built from 1675, was designed by Sir Christopher Wren. William the Conqueror began the building of the Tower of London in 1078 and as well as being a prison and place of torture and execution, it has served as a royal palace. Tower Bridge was opened in 1894, and since then the only major change has been the installation of electrical motors to lift the two massive central spans of the drawbridge.

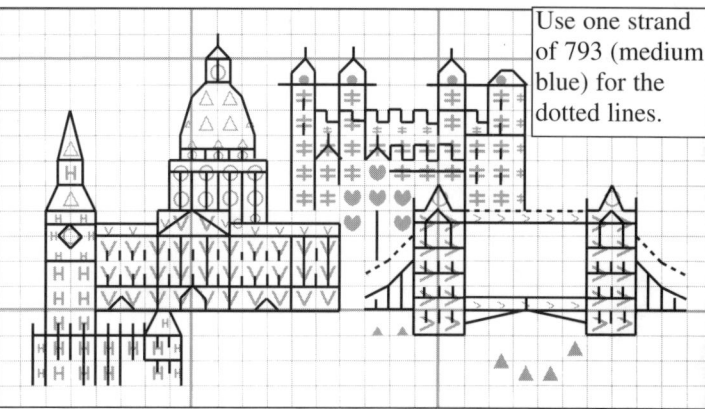

Use one strand of 793 (medium blue) for the dotted lines.

Home of the Archbishops of Canterbury since the 12th century, Lambeth Palace stands across the river from the King's Palace at Westminster.

To the east of the City lie London's former Docklands, now being developed as apartments, offices and leisure facilities.

At Greenwich pier the 'Cutty Sark' lies moored in a dry dock. This beautiful ship with its tall masts was built in 1869 as a tea clipper, carrying precious cargoes between Britain and the Orient. Moored nearby is the 'Gypsy Moth', the tiny yacht in which Sir Francis Chichester made the first single-handed circumnavigation of the globe in 1966-7.

The Royal Naval College, Greenwich, was originally built as a hospital for infirm and aged seamen, but is now used for officer training. In the centre, behind the College, is the Queen's House, the central building of the National Maritime Museum. High on the hill above Greenwich is the Old Royal Observatory.

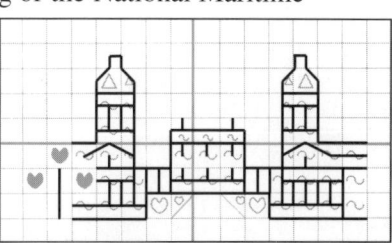

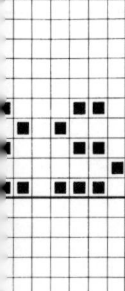

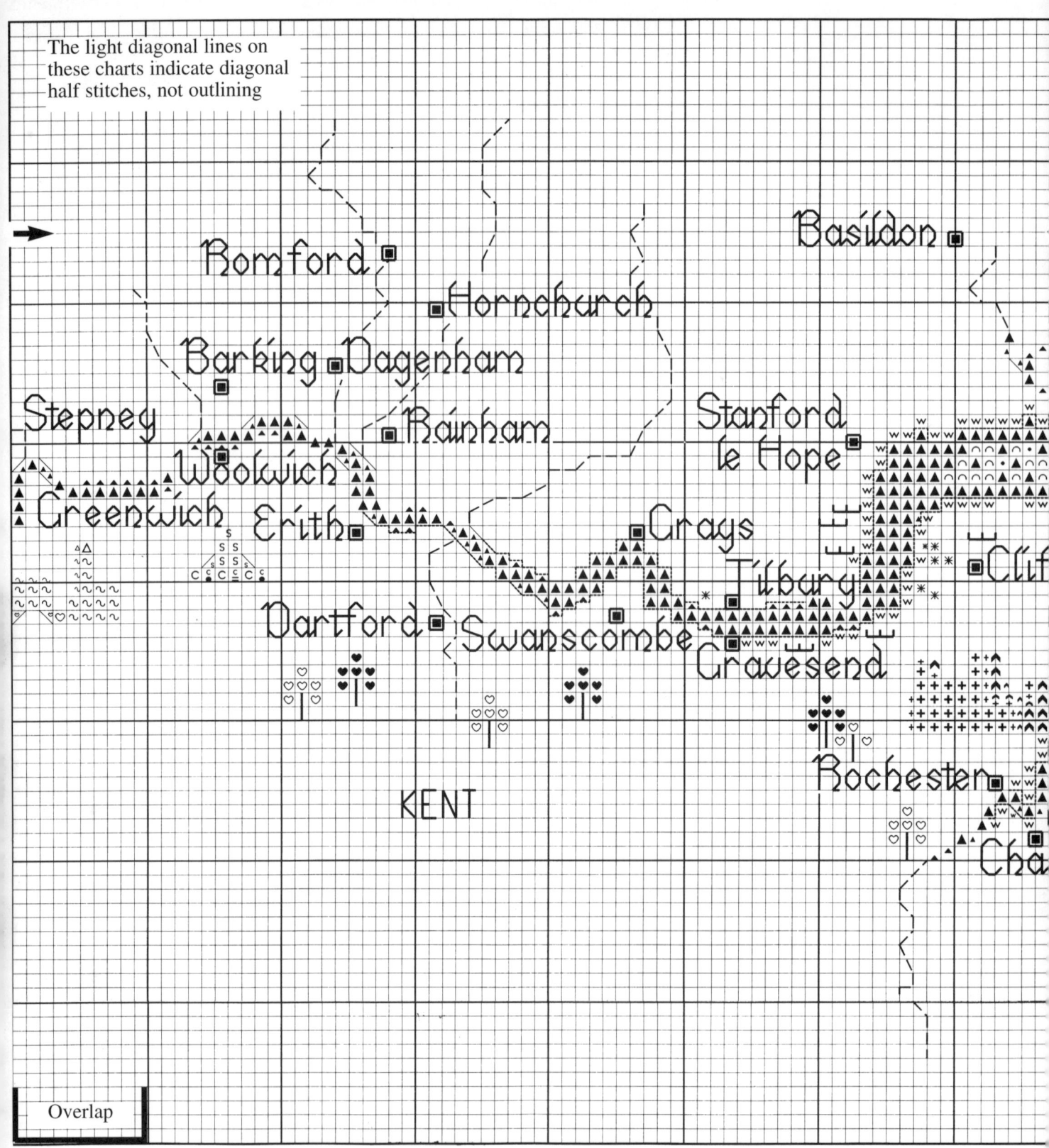

The light diagonal lines on these charts indicate diagonal half stitches, not outlining

Overlap

Cross stitch using two strands of cotton
- ■ 310 (black)
- = 402 (copper)
- △ 415 (med. blue grey)
- × 453 (light red grey)
- ▲ 640 (dk. brown grey)
- + 644 (lt. brown grey)
- ● 646 (dark grey)
- c 738 (gold)
- ▲ 792 (dark blue)
- ∩ 793 (medium blue)
- s 3072 (lt. grey)

- ♥ 3347 (med. green)
- ♡ 3348 (light green)
- ○ White

Using one strand of cotton
- ✱ 792 (dark blue)
- · 794 (light blue)
- w 841 (medium pink brown)

Cross stitch using one strand of each of two colours
- ∿ 3072 (lt. grey) and white

Outlining for lettering
One strand of 310

Outlining for rivers
------ one strand of 792
_____ two strands of 792

Outlining for buildings
One strand of 844

Outlining for tree trunks
Two strands of 3021

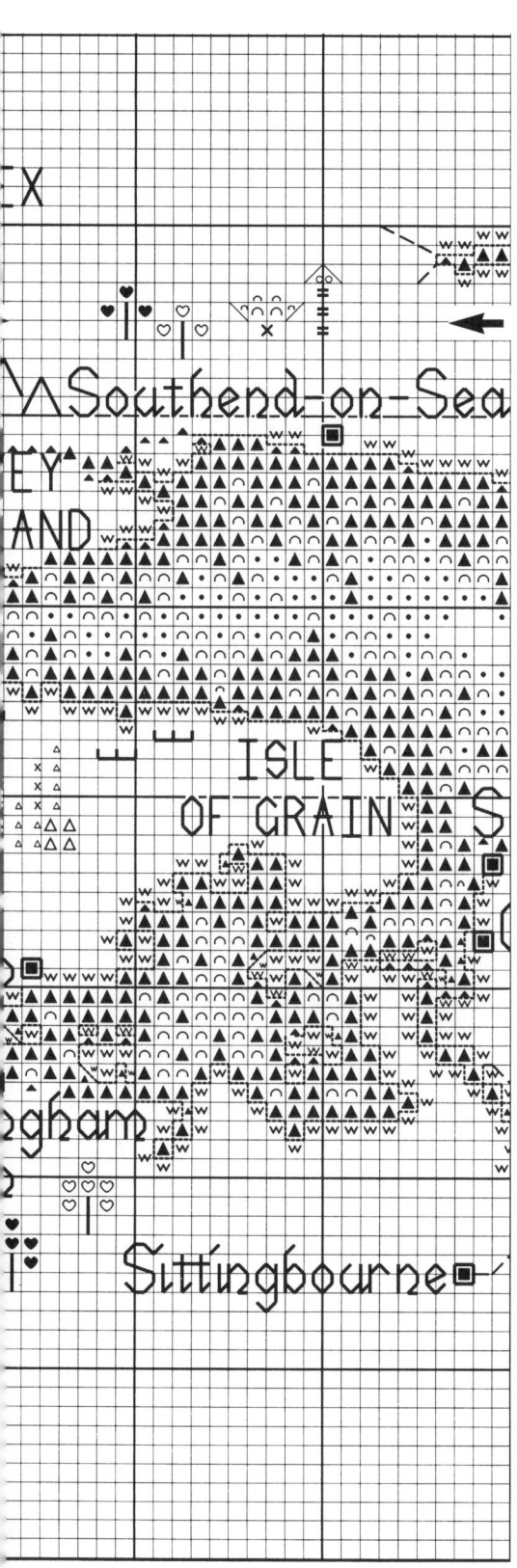

The River Thames from Woolwich to Southend-on-Sea

Because sea levels around Britain, particularly in the south-east, are gradually rising it was necessary to construct the Thames Barrier at Woolwich. This protects London from the danger of flooding.

Most of the fine buildings at Woolwich, such as the Royal Military Academy and the Royal Artillery Barracks, were designed for army use. The Rotunda, which is pictured here, was designed by John Nash as a temporary pavilion for the Prince Regent in St. James's Park in 1814. It was rebuilt at Woolwich after the Battle of Waterloo when it housed some of the spoils of victory. It is now a museum showing the evolution of the gun.

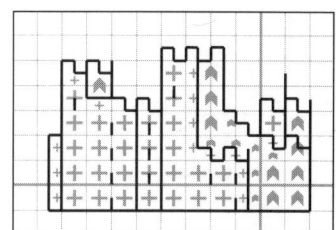

A passenger ferry runs from Gravesend to Tilbury. At St. George's Church, Gravesend lies the grave of the Red Indian Princess Pocahontas.

The fort at Tilbury was built by King Henry VIII in 1539, and it was here in 1588 that Queen Elizabeth I reviewed the army raised to resist the Armada.

The ancient cathedral city of Rochester stands on the lower reaches of the River Medway. The crossing over the Medway, on the route from Dover to London, gave the city its early strategic importance.

Rochester Castle is pictured on the map. It dates from shortly after the Norman Conquest, and was built on a site which had been fortified by the Romans and the Saxons to defend the Medway crossing.

Rochester is closely associated with the novelist Charles Dickens.

Cooling Marshes, the land on the Kentish shore west of the Isle of Grain, has changed little for many centuries. Here the Romney Marsh breed of sheep, or Kents, graze undisturbed.

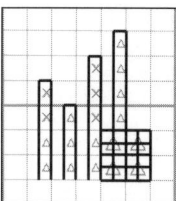

The Isle of Grain oil refinery stands to the east of Cooling Marshes. It was opened by BP in the 1950s, taking crude oil from the Middle East and more recently the North Sea, and refining it to provide petrol, fuels, lubricants and tar. In 1981 the refinery was closed due to the fall in demand for industrial fuels.

In the 18th century Southend-on-Sea was an oyster fishery. It became a holiday town after the Prince Regent made sea-bathing fashionable. Being within easy reach of day-trippers from the East End of London, Southend was a popular seaside resort during the 19th century and early decades of the 20th century.

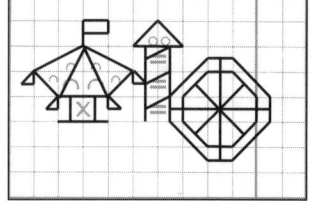

Outlining for Hills
/\ two strands of 301

Coastline working in backstitch
------- one strand of 839 (brown)

Marshland working in backstitch
⊔⊔ two strands of 935 (dark green)

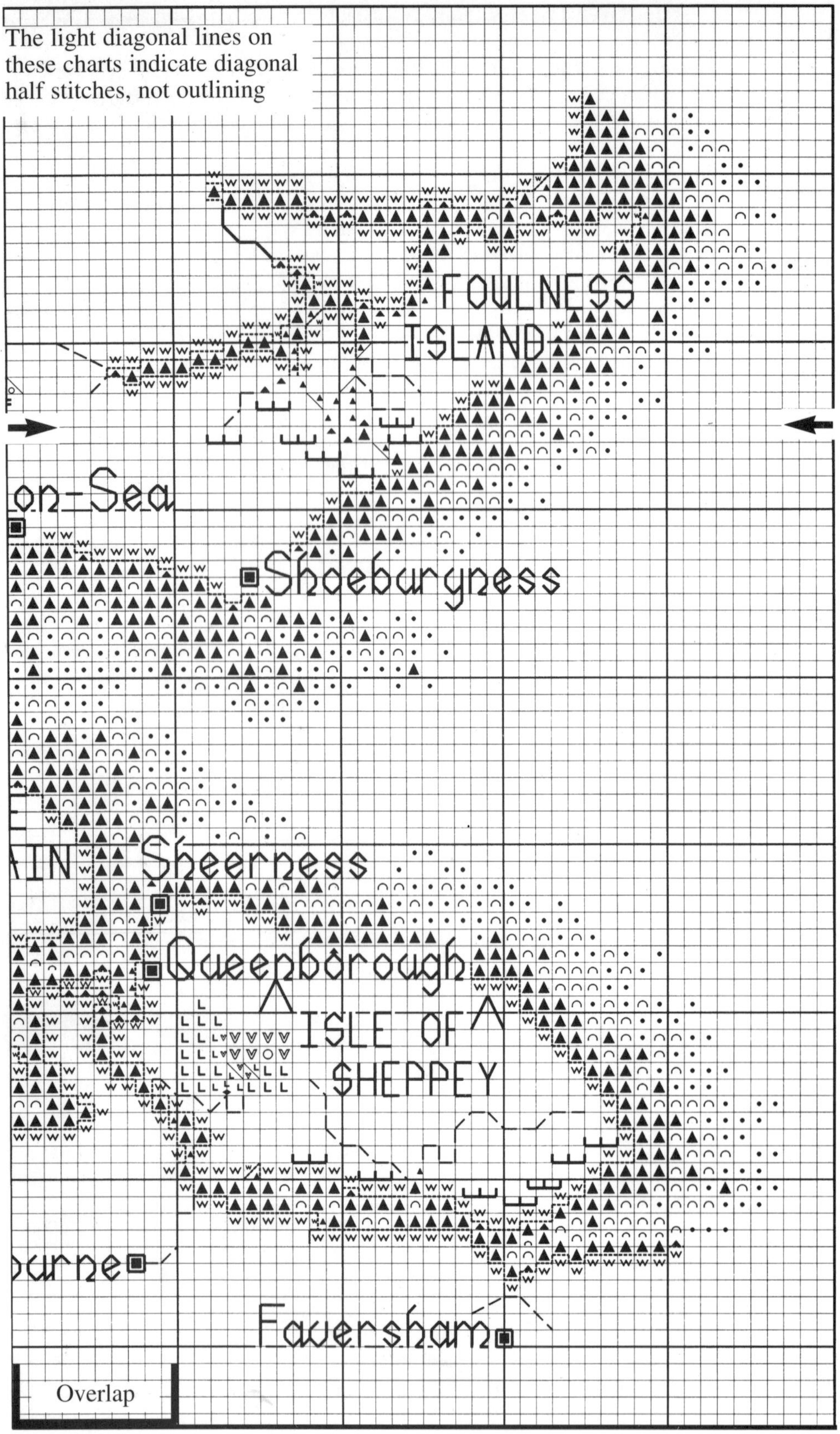
The light diagonal lines on these charts indicate diagonal half stitches, not outlining
FOULNESS ISLAND
on-Sea
Shoeburyness
IN
Sheerness
Queenborough
ISLE OF SHEPPEY
ourne
Faversham
Overlap

The mouth of the River Thames

The Isle of Sheppey means 'island of sheep'. There has been a dockyard at Sheerness on the Isle of Sheppey since 1665. Samuel Pepys supervised its construction. However, much of the present dockyard was designed by John Rennie in 1812. Formerly it was a naval dockyard but since 1960 it has become a thriving commercial port.

The town of Queenborough, together with a castle, was built by Edward III in the late 14th century to guard the Medway estuary. Its name is taken from Queen Philippa, his wife.

The castle has gone, but the church is pictured on the map.

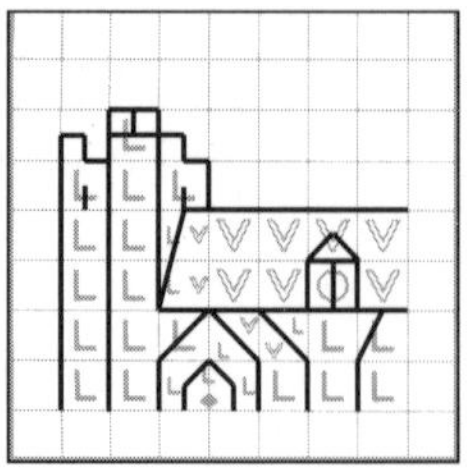

Cross stitch using two strands of cotton
- ■ 310 (black)
- ▲ 792 (dark blue)
- ∩ 793 (med. blue)
- ◆ 844 (charcoal)
- ○ White

Using one strand of cotton
- ✱ 792 (dark blue)
- • 794 (light blue)
- w 841 (med. pink brown)

Cross stitch using one strand of each of two colours
- V 647 (grey) and 3064 (red brown)
- L 648 (med. grey) and white

Outlining for Lettering
One strand of 310

Outlining for Rivers
------one strand of 792
———two strands of 792

Oulining for Buildings
One strand of 844

Outlining for Hills
/\ two strands of 301

Coastline working in back stitch
-------one strand of 839 (brown)

Marshland working in backstitch
ꟾꟾꟾ two strands of 935 (dark green)